CW01512633

Original title:
Mirrors of the Eternal Abyss

Copyright © 2025 Swan Charm
All rights reserved.

Author: Johan Kirsipuu
ISBN HARDBACK: 978-1-80561-389-3
ISBN PAPERBACK: 978-1-80561-950-5

Shadows Beneath Time's Surface

In the whisper of dusk, shadows play,
Echoes of moments that fade away.
Time weaves its cloth with threads of gray,
Beneath the surface, dreams lay in sway.

Silent reflections, memories intertwine,
Each heartbeat echoes, a fragile line.
Waves of the past in a gentle sign,
Shadows dance softly, as stars align.

Fragments of the Unfathomable

Scattered like leaves in the autumn breeze,
Fragments of thoughts drift, seeking to please.
Hidden beneath layers, our minds tease,
Unfathomable depths, where silence frees.

The puzzle of being, in pieces we find,
Whispers of echoes, our hearts intertwined.
In shadows of reason, we search and rewind,
Fragments of truth, a journey unkind.

Echoing Silence of the Depths

In the stillness of night, silence screams,
Echoes of longing, unspoken dreams.
Depths of the heart hold secrets it seems,
A quiet abyss where no light redeems.

Beneath the calm surface, storms can arise,
In the heart's depths, uncertainty lies.
Echoing silence beneath darkened skies,
Each whisper of hope in the stillness cries.

Gaze into the Endless Chasm

Gaze into the chasm, fathomless dark,
Where shadows converge and lost dreams embark.
Endless horizons ignite a spark,
The abyss calls softly, a haunting lark.

The soul's silent journey, fearless and grand,
Facing the depths, we struggle to stand.
In endless chasms, we learn to expand,
The echoes of courage, within us withstand.

Simplicity of the Dark Depths

In shadows deep, where silence keeps,
Whispers dance and secrets weep.
The night reveals its subtle grace,
In quiet corners, we find our place.

A single spark, a fleeting glow,
Guides the heart where few will go.
Embrace the dark, let worries part,
In simplicity, we find our art.

The depths invite, with arms so wide,
To mystery and peace inside.
In stillness, truths begin to flow,
The beauty found in the dark's warm glow.

Glimpses Through the Shattered Veil

Beyond the veil, where shadows play,
Glimpses spark in the disarray.
Fragments glow, like stars in night,
Truths emerge, bathed in light.

Within despair, hope flickers bright,
A shattered world, yet full of sight.
Through cracks we see, a story told,
Of warmth and warmth in the bitter cold.

Lost in dreams, the past awakes,
Each shard of life, a chance that breaks.
In every fracture, a chance to feel,
Hope surrounds us, a gentle seal.

The Depth's Dark Revelations

In depths unknown, where secrets dwell,
Echoes weave a silent spell.
With every breath, the truth unfolds,
In shadows deep, the heart beholds.

The tension builds, the depths arise,
In watery gaze, we find our ties.
Revelations born from darker seas,
Awakened dreams on whispered breeze.

Each thought a wave, each pulse a tide,
Steering ships where hopes reside.
Upon the brink, we dare to dive,
In darkness, we continually strive.

The Abyss Unfurls Its Secrets

In every shadow lies a tale,
As the abyss begins to unveil.
From depths profound, memories wake,
Each moment cherished, the heart's own ache.

The vast expanse, both wild and free,
Holds secrets waiting just for me.
To journey forth in quiet trust,
In the abyss, reveal we must.

With every breath, the mysteries bloom,
Transforming fear into a room.
To dance with the dark, embrace the night,
In the abyss, we find our light.

Shadows of Timeless Whispers

In corners dark, where dreams reside,
Echoes dance, and fears collide.
Fleeting moments slip through time,
Softly weaving into rhyme.

Footsteps linger, shadows play,
Silent voices guide the way.
Each secret held, a story spun,
In whispered tones, the past begun.

Through twilight's veil, a path unfurls,
Where ancient tales of life entwirl.
In twilight's grip, we find our ground,
In stillness deep, a truth profound.

Shadows cast by moonlit gleam,
Carry forth the silent dream.
In every sigh, a memory bends,
With every breath, the past transcends.

In the quiet, we take flight,
Chasing shadows into night.
Timeless whispers echo still,
In our hearts, a restless thrill.

The Boundless Mirrorscapes

Reflections ripple in endless streams,
Where light and shadow weave like dreams.
A world unfolds in fractured glass,
Endless layers of moments pass.

Echoes of laughter intertwine,
In this realm where stars align.
Each glance reveals a hidden maze,
In mirrors bright, we lose our gaze.

Time stretches thin, a silver thread,
Connecting all the words unsaid.
In every face, a story glows,
A tapestry where wonder flows.

Through shifting scenes, we walk and weave,
In this space where we believe.
Fragments swirl, a dance of fate,
In boundless depths, we navigate.

Mirrors reflect our souls' intent,
In silence, dreams are truly bent.
With every step, new visions light,
In mirrorscapes, we take to flight.

Embrace of the Abyssal Depths

In ocean's cradle, shadows deep,
Where secrets dwell and stillness keeps.
The heartbeats echo, soft and slow,
In endless waters, tides will flow.

Whispers rise from depths unknown,
In trembling waves, the truth is sown.
Each sigh of currents pulls us near,
To depths where dreams and fears appear.

In the abyss, we find our breath,
A paradox of life and death.
With every plunge, we confront the night,
In the dark, we search for light.

Beneath the surface, worlds collide,
With every stroke, the ocean's tide.
The embrace of depths, a gentle grip,
In salty waters, we take the trip.

Through fluid realms, we drift and sway,
In darkened blue, the night turns gray.
The abyss calls with endless grace,
In depths unknown, we find our place.

Visions Beyond the Void

In the silence where shadows creep,
Visions stir from restless sleep.
Beyond the veil, the galaxies spin,
In cosmic dance, we find within.

Starlit paths lead to dreams untold,
In realms where mysteries unfold.
Each spark of light a thought released,\nWithin the void,
our souls are pleased.

Echoes of time flash in the dark,
In every whisper, a distant spark.
Through nothingness, we glimpse our fate,
In visions grand, we contemplate.

Floating freely, we rise and soar,
Through boundless realms, evermore.
In the vastness, we learn to breathe,
In the silence, we find reprieve.

Beyond the void, the echoes sing,
Of hopes and dreams on angel's wing.
In ethereal light, visions bloom,
In the vast unknown, we find our room.

Veils of the Perpetual Night

In shadows deep where silence dwells,
The stars are caught in whispered spells.
A cloak of dusk, a tender sigh,
Beneath the darkened velvet sky.

A moonlit path, a fleeting gaze,
Where lost souls wander in the haze.
Time drifts by on feathered wing,
Embracing all the night can bring.

Echoes weave through tangled dreams,
And stitch the heart with moonlight seams.
Each breath a pulse, a quiet song,
The night, a place where we belong.

In every corner, secrets creep,
As shadows cradle those who weep.
Veils murmur tales of love and dread,
In the embrace of stars long fled.

Secrets Woven in Darkness

Beneath the veil where secrets lie,
Darkness dances, whispers sigh.
Threads of fate in silence spun,
Hidden paths where night is begun.

In corners dim, the shadows play,
Marking time that slips away.
An echo calls from deep within,
Awakening the light of sin.

The tapestry of night unfolds,
In webs of dreams, the truth beholds.
Step by step, the heart draws near,
To unravel every hidden fear.

Each heartbeat thrums a secret tune,
Beneath the watchful, patient moon.
In every whisper, every breath,
Lies the dance of life and death.

The Abyss Gazes Back

Into the void where silence reigns,
A shadowed gaze that still remains.
Reflection caught in depths so vast,
What lies beyond the present past?

Fingers trace the edges bare,
Of thoughts that linger in the air.
A promise made, a longing thought,
What fervent hope the abyss wrought?

In darkness deep, the silence speaks,
Each fleeting moment hides and seeks.
A mirror cold, the gaze shall hold,
The secrets of the brave and bold.

What dreams reside in blackest night?
What fears embrace the fading light?
Each soul exposed, a glimpse of fate,
In the abyss, we contemplate.

Illusions of the Infinite Abyss

Gazing deep into the infinite,
Where shadows merge and time must sit.
A tapestry of stars unfolds,
In visions bright, our dreams are sold.

Reflections twist and turn like smoke,
In every glimpse, our hearts are broke.
What lies beyond the edge of thought?
In that silence, battles fought.

The pull of darkness weaves a thread,
Binding hopes that go unsaid.
Illusions dance, a spectral waltz,
In the silence, echoing faults.

Within the void, the mind may roam,
Yet yearns for warmth, a place called home.
What stories wait in the abyss?
A haunting call, a lover's kiss.

Beneath the Still Waters

Whispers echo soft and low,
Beneath the tide where secrets flow.
A world so calm, a hidden grace,
Reflections trapped in a liquid space.

Shadows dance with gentle ease,
Ripples play beneath the trees.
Fish glide by in silent flight,
Beneath the stillness, hidden light.

Memories drift like fallen leaves,
Carried forth by quiet heaves.
Each movement stirs the glassy skin,
A silent tale, where dreams begin.

Lost in depth, the heart does yearn,
For treasures found, for lessons learned.
The world above, a distant song,
Beneath the waters, I belong.

In the depths, the truth is known,
In every wave, a seed is sown.
Life flows forth, like a gentle stream,
Beneath the still waters, we dream.

Lurking in the Periphery

Shadows linger just out of sight,
Veiled in whispers of fading light.
Eyes that watch from hidden nooks,
Heartbeats echo in quiet books.

Figures move in the corner's glance,
Dancing just beyond our chance.
Secrets held in a breathless sigh,
Nothing certain, yet we comply.

Every flicker, every chill,
Hints of presence, eerie thrill.
A pull towards the unknown fate,
As we tread and contemplate.

The world spins in a twisted maze,
Familiar yet caught in a daze.
What waits beyond our simple view?
Is it comfort, or fear anew?

In shadows played by muted light,
Lurking figures clutch the night.
What beckons us to look away?
The unknown calls, where doubt will stay.

Dreams Intertwined with Darkness

In the stillness, shadows creep,
Dreams entwined in the depths of sleep.
Visions swirl in a dusky haze,
Where light is veiled in a mournful phase.

Threads of hope, like gossamer,
Weave through fears, they gently stir.
A dance of thoughts, both dark and bright,
In the silence of the night.

Whispers echo through the void,
As hidden dreams lie unalloyed.
The heart bears witness to the scheme,
As shadows play, I chase the dream.

Waking moments tiptoe near,
Fleeting glimpses of buried fear.
In dreams' embrace, we seek the light,
Yet lost we wander, deep in night.

Threads we pull, with careful hands,
Intertwined in forgotten lands.
Where darkness reigns, a flicker's grace,
Awaits the dawn, our dreams embrace.

Cracks in the Fabric of Time

Moments fracture, split apart,
Echoes linger, leaving a mark.
Time slips through like fine sand grains,
Fraying edges, lost refrains.

Days collide in strange ballet,
Past and future softly sway.
Muffled voices call out, unseen,
In the seams where fate has been.

Hidden paths of what might have been,
Crisscrossed dreams in a faded grin.
Threads unravel, stories blend,
Time's illusion never ends.

In these fissures, we find light,
Tales of sorrow, moments bright.
Whispers of what we cannot see,
Cracks in time whisper to me.

Lost in fragments, we learn to soar,
Time is a window, an endless door.
With every leap through the fleeting night,
We shape our fate, we seek the light.

Chasing the Fleeting Echo

In shadows cast by evening light,
We wander paths of whispered night.
Chasing echoes that softly fade,
In dreams of what was never made.

With every step, a fleeting sound,
A ghost of joy that can't be found.
We reach for whispers lost in time,
Like notes of a forgotten rhyme.

The stars above begin to dance,
Their light a fleeting, fragile chance.
We trace the outlines of the past,
A fleeting echo, fading fast.

In twilight's arms, we seek the spark,
Of memories bright that left a mark.
The echoes linger, soft and sweet,
Yet drift away on starlit feet.

So let us chase what once was near,
A fragile tune, a whispered cheer.
In every echo, hope's embrace,
We find the pulse of time and space.

The Depths of Unspeakable Thought

In silence deep, where shadows dwell,
Lie whispers of a hidden spell.
Thoughts entwined like vines that creep,
Into the corners where secrets sleep.

The mind a labyrinth, vast and wide,
With echoes of the heart inside.
We dive beneath the surface gray,
To find the truths that fade away.

Each pondered thought, a swirling tide,
Where reason sinks and dreams abide.
We swim through currents dark and deep,
And in that depth, our secrets keep.

Yet in the dark, a spark ignites,
A flicker born from silent nights.
It pulls us forth, through murky haze,
To glimpse the light beyond the maze.

So dare to seek what lies below,
In depths where restless feelings flow.
To speak the thoughts we dare not share,
And find the beauty hiding there.

The Abyssal Silence Speaks

In silence deep, the shadows stir,
With whispers soft, they start to purr.
The abyss awakens, void yet bright,
With secrets held beyond our sight.

It speaks in echoes, faint but clear,
In every moment, always near.
A language formed from dark's embrace,
A dance of time, a quiet grace.

The stillness hums with ancient lore,
Of dreams long lost, and opened doors.
In depths where silence weaves its thread,
It paints the canvas of the dead.

The void, a mirror to the soul,
Reflects our fears, makes us whole.
In darkened corners, truths arise,
Veiled in shadows, they seek the skies.

So listen close, let silence seep,
Into your heart, where secrets keep.
For in the silence, wisdom hides,
And in the abyss, love abides.

Relics of the Starlit Abyss

In twilight's grasp, the stars align,
Relics lost in space and time.
Each twinkle whispers tales untold,
Of ancient dreams and treasures bold.

The cosmos holds its breath in awe,
As we unveil the night's raw law.
Beneath the veil of space's glow,
We find the seeds of what we sow.

A journey marked by light and dark,
In every star, a vibrant spark.
Relics scattered through the void,
With every wish, our hearts enjoyed.

We reach beyond the known expanse,
In starlit depths, we find our chance.
To gather whispers from the stars,
And hold their light, despite the scars.

So let us wander through the night,
Embrace the relics, share their light.
For in the starlit abyss we roam,
We find our fate, we find our home.

Resonances from the Veil of Night

The stars whisper tales of old,
Casting dreams in silver bold.
Moonlight dances, soft and bright,
Emerging secrets of the night.

In shadows deep where silence lies,
A symphony beneath the skies.
Echoes linger, time stands still,
As hearts awaken to the thrill.

Winds that carry voices near,
Speak of hopes and hidden fear.
Softly woven in the air,
Mysteries hide with gentle care.

Beneath the cloak of darkened hue,
A world unfolds, both old and new.
Resonances dance in twilight's hold,
Stories in the night retold.

Here in the hush, dreams intertwine,
Connecting souls like threads divine.
Embrace the night, let your spirit soar,
In resonances, find your core.

The Silent Call of the Deep

In ocean's arms, the silence sings,
A call to depths where freedom clings.
Waves of whispers tug and pull,
A siren's song, both soft and full.

Beneath the surface, shadows play,
In restless currents, they drift away.
Secrets hidden in the blue,
Waiting for hearts that dare to pursue.

Moonlit tides, they rise and fall,
Resonating with the deep's enthrall.
The pulse of life, a rhythmic beat,
In the silent call, our spirits meet.

Bubbles rise like fleeting dreams,
In darkened depths, magic gleams.
Listen closely, let it seep,
The wonders held in silence deep.

Explore the vast, the unknown trail,
In the quiet depths, hear the veil.
The ocean's heart will always keep,
A gentle peace—a silent leap.

Lament in the Darkened Waters

A shadowed hush falls on the sea,
Where sorrow whispers softly, free.
Echoes linger in the dark,
Silent tears leave their mark.

The moonlight casts a fleeting glow,
On waves that weep what none can show.
In shadows deep, grief finds its way,
In darkened waters where memories sway.

Lost in currents, drift the sighs,
Each ripple carries soft goodbyes.
A lament sung beneath the tide,
In every heartbeat, life's divide.

The depths conceal both pain and grace,
As time flows on, we find our place.
Through the murky veil we glean,
The beauty found in what has been.

Yet in the dark, a glimmer stays,
Hope's gentle light in shattered bays.
In every lament, a song anew,
In darkened waters, we push through.

Refractions of the Shadowed Mind

In realms where thought begins to wane,
Echoes flicker like hidden flame.
Thoughts collide, a shifting dance,
In shadowed corners, minds enhance.

Reflections twist, they bend and break,
Dreams like ripples, softly shake.
In the depths of consciousness,
Reside the fears we must address.

Fragments of light weave tales of gray,
In blurred reflections, we drift away.
Chasing shadows of what may be,
In silent thoughts, we seek to see.

Through murky waters of the brain,
Find clarity amid the pain.
A spark ignites in twilight's hour,
Transforming doubt into pure power.

So in the mind, let colors blend,
In shadowed depths, our visions mend.
Refractions lead to brighter skies,
Where understanding finally lies.

Threads of the Cosmic Void

In the dark, we weave our dreams,
Stars awaken, bursting seams.
Galaxies dance, a cosmic loom,
Threads of light dispel the gloom.

Whispers echo through the night,
A tapestry of endless flight.
Woven tales of time and space,
In the void, we find our place.

Nebulas swirl in vibrant hues,
Painting paths of ancient clues.
Through the silence, visions call,
In the cosmic, we find our all.

Tides of Nightfall Secrets

As dusk descends, the shadows creep,
Secrets stir from twilight's deep.
Beneath the stars, whispers sigh,
In the tides of night, dreams lie.

The moonlight casts a silver glow,
Over waters, restless flow.
Ripples holding tales untold,
In their depths, the night is bold.

Softly sung by the winds that weep,
Ancient echoes, secrets keep.
In the dark, the heart can roam,
In the nightfall, we find home.

Illuminated Descent into the Deep

Into the depths, we bravely dive,
In the silence, shadows thrive.
Bioluminescent dreams take flight,
Illuminated by the night.

Coral gardens, vibrant and rare,
Whispering secrets in salty air.
Currents pulse like a beating heart,
In the deep, we play our part.

With each wave, a story unfolds,
In liquid depths, the brave are bold.
We discover worlds beyond our own,
In the depths, our spirits are sown.

The Silent Abyss Beckons

In the silence, shadows grow,
The abyss calls, a soft echo.
Darkness waits, patient and wide,
With open arms, it draws inside.

Ancient whispers in the chill,
Mysteries waiting to fulfill.
The deeper we go, the more we find,
In the abyss, we leave behind.

Lost in twilight, forever we roam,
In the depths, we seek our home.
The silent call, a soothing tone,
In the abyss, we are not alone.

Echos of Forgotten Dreams

Whispers fade in empty halls,
Memories dance with shadowed calls.
Once bright flames now dimmed and pale,
Lost in time, they start to wail.

Ghostly laughter haunts the night,
Fleeting visions dimming light.
Fractured tales of love and loss,
In the silence, they emboss.

A glimpse of what once felt so real,
Broken hopes that never heal.
Each dream a thread now torn apart,
Echoes linger in the heart.

Searching through the fog of years,
Carrying both joy and tears.
Every whisper, every sigh,
A reminder of days gone by.

Yet in shadows, sparks can glow,
Through the darkness, seeds we sow.
In forgotten dreams, we find
Fragments of the heart, entwined.

Fragments in the Twilight Pool

Beneath the stars, the water glows,
Reflecting dreams, the twilight shows.
Silken ripples, soft and light,
Whispers linger through the night.

Shattered pieces in the deep,
Silent stories long to keep.
Every drop a world unseen,
Fragments of where we have been.

Time stands still in gentle waves,
Pulling hearts from ancient graves.
In this twilight, shadows play,
Promises of a new dawn's ray.

Glimmers catch the passing breeze,
A soft touch among the trees.
In the stillness, hopes appear,
Murmuring what we hold dear.

Throw your dreams upon the surface,
Let them swim without purpose.
In this pool, all fears dissolve,
In fragments, our souls evolve.

The Haunting Beneath the Surface

Deep within the silent lake,
Lies a secret, soft and raked.
Fingers trail the chilling foam,
Hiding fears we call our home.

Echoing voices from below,
Whispers of a world we know.
Lingering doubts in the depths lay,
Yearning for the light of day.

A shimmer breaks the surface calm,
Like a tale spun with a balm.
Regrets rise like vapor's breath,
Fleeting shadows dance with death.

Searching hearts dive to explore,
Haunted dreams we can't ignore.
Glances fleeting, moments lost,
In the deep, we bear the cost.

What lies hidden in the dark?
Fleeting glimpses of a spark.
Through the depths, our spirits creep,
Haunting whispers, secrets keep.

Beneath the Surface of Dreams

Awake in a realm where shadows play,
Where endless night meets the day.
Beneath the veil, the silence breathes,
In quiet corners, our heart believes.

Threads of color twist and twine,
In the fabric, secrets align.
Beneath the surface, visions stir,
Stories waiting to recur.

Each soft sigh a moment known,
A place where seeds of hope are sown.
With every turn, the heart takes flight,
In the dreaming, we find light.

Ripples dance in starlit seas,
Carried on a gentle breeze.
Beneath the surface, time stands still,
Awakening a dormant will.

So let us wander through the night,
Into the depths, where dreams ignite.
In shadows cast and whispers found,
Beneath the surface, love is crowned.

The Silent Abyss Within

In the shadowed corners hold,
Whispers echo, secrets told.
Hearts conceal their haunting pain,
Silent cries like falling rain.

Depths of thought begin to swell,
In the stillness, stories dwell.
Fears entwined, like roots of trees,
Drawing breath on trembling knees.

Memories like ghostly hands,
Reach for solace, where it stands.
A void stretches, vast and wide,
No light shines to pierce inside.

Beneath calm lies tremors' force,
Churning tides on hidden course.
Hope flickers like a distant flame,
Yearning still to stake its claim.

Rise from silence, voice the plight,
Find the strength to seek the light.
For within the darkest space,
Lies the heart's elaborate grace.

Sins of the Starlit Depths

Underneath a velvet sky,
Whispers of the lost comply.
Stars, they blink with tales untold,
Of the hearts that drift like gold.

Echoes of a world once bright,
Now twisted in the shrouded night.
Lust and greed in starlit gleam,
Pull us deeper, lost in dream.

Waves of shadows, sins awake,
Caress the soul with every quake.
The depths hold stories steeped in dread,
Where light once shone, now fear is bred.

Falling deeper, no retreat,
Chained to darkness, incomplete.
Yet within this vast expanse,
Hope still dares to take a chance.

In the void, we search for peace,
Longing for the shadows' cease.
Stars will guide through wars we fight,
To find warmth within the night.

Shards of Darkness and Light

Fragments glimmer in the night,
Dance of shadows, burst of light.
Both entwined in twisted fate,
A silent war we contemplate.

Turning points and paths collide,
In our hearts, where fears reside.
Each shard tells a different tale,
Of the hopes that often frail.

Darkness preys where light was bright,
In the depths, a constant fight.
Yet the beams, though weak, persist,
Through despair, they still exist.

Choices made beneath the stars,
Breaking through the countless bars.
In this clash of night and day,
Dreams emerge, not swept away.

Through the storm, we find the way,
Shards of light, a bright display.
In each fracture, beauty grows,
In the complexity, one knows.

The Deep's Lament

In the silence, echoes mourn,
Stories fraught with hearts that scorn.
Waves of sorrow kiss the shore,
As shadows whisper evermore.

Voices lost beneath the waves,
Carry tales of restless graves.
Each tide takes with it a dream,
Leaving behind a haunting theme.

Beneath the foam, a world cries,
Filling with unvoiced goodbyes.
In the depth, the shades surround,
Yearning for a way to sound.

Hope submerged in endless night,
Flickers dim, but holds on tight.
Sorrow dances with the sea,
In every drop, a memory.

Yet the depths, with pain replete,
Still hold beauty bittersweet.
For in loss, we find our song,
A truth shared, where we belong.

Abyssal Visions

In the depths where shadows play,
Whispers dance in a silent sway.
Dreams emerge from the ocean's hold,
Tales of wonders, yet untold.

Eyes like stars in the murky sea,
Glimmers of truths, they long to be.
Vast abyss, dark and wide,
Secrets lost in the shifting tide.

Figures swirl in the depths below,
Fractured light in a clandestine show.
Phantom echoes call the brave,
In this abyss, they seek to save.

Through liquid voids, visions creep,
In blackened silence, secrets keep.
A world unseen, a haunting grace,
With every pulse, a soft embrace.

Fear not the dark, embrace the night,
For in shadows, there's hidden light.
Abyssal visions, vast and grand,
A journey deep, just take my hand.

The Unseen Reflections

In mirrored depths where echoes dwell,
Mysteries hide, and shadows swell.
Fragments of dreams in twilight's cast,
Waves of silence from the past.

Ghostly images float and tease,
Caught in whispers of the breeze.
Reality bends in this hush,
In unmade thoughts, we feel the rush.

Fleeting glimpses of what was known,
Time's soft touch, forever sown.
Beyond the glass, a world untamed,
In unseen reflections, we're not blamed.

Voices linger in stillness clear,
Calling softly, drawing near.
Through veils of mist and laced with light,
We wander lost in the endless night.

In shadows cast, the truth will gleam,
In unseen reflections, share the dream.
We walk the line of the known and unknown,
In this realm, we find our home.

Through the Veil of Night

Stars reflect in the calm below,
Whispers drift on a gentler flow.
Through the veil, the mysteries gleam,
Silent night holds a timeless dream.

The dark embraces every sigh,
Beneath the moon, our spirits fly.
Colors fade into the mist,
In this hour, all shadows twist.

Cloth of darkness, soft and fine,
We trace the paths where dreams align.
Echoes of footsteps in the night,
Haunting tales blend wrong with right.

Through the veil, the stories weave,
In twilight's embrace, we learn to believe.
Each breath a secret, deeply held,
In night's enchantment, we are compelled.

Underneath the canvas of stars,
We wander free, defying scars.
Through the veil, our visions blaze,
In night's embrace, we find our ways.

Chasing the Lightless

In the corners where shadows lie,
Hopes like shadows learn to sigh.
Chasing dreams that slip away,
In the void, we yearn to stay.

Timeless echoes fill the air,
Fractured visions, a whispered prayer.
The lightless paths twist and coil,
In flickering thoughts, our minds embroil.

Wanderers seek in the shrouded black,
Finding solace, we can't turn back.
The glow of dawn is out of reach,
Yet in the dark, we learn to teach.

Fleeting chances, moments passed,
Through the quiet, shadows cast.
In lightless corners, secrets lay,
As we chase the night into day.

Within the dark, courage grows bold,
In chasing dreams, our stories unfold.
Lightless whispers, we won't dismiss,
For in the chase, we find our bliss.

Fractured Dreams Beneath the Surface

In shadows cast by fading light,
Sleepless whispers haunt the night.
Fragments of a wistful song,
Echoes where the lost belong.

Waves crash down on crumbling hopes,
Tides that pull at tangled ropes.
Beneath the calm, a restless heart,
Yearns to mend what fell apart.

Reflections shimmer, dreams collide,
In the depths where feelings hide.
Silhouettes of what once was clear,
Dissolve in currents, disappear.

Moonlit paths through murky skies,
Guide the souls that dream and sigh.
Fractured visions softly gleam,
Dancing in a fleeting dream.

Awake, yet drifting like the sea,
Chasing shadows, never free.
The surface glows, yet darkness weaves,
Fractured dreams that no one leaves.

Luminous Echoes of the Deep

In azure depths where silence sings,
Luminous whispers, gentle wings.
Echoes of a past so bright,
Flickers lost in endless night.

Rippling waves of thoughts so clear,
Casting shadows, drawing near.
Underneath the tranquil hue,
Voices call, and hearts pursue.

Secrets veiled in liquid grace,
Bubbles rise, a fleeting trace.
Galaxies in each embrace,
Holding time, a sacred space.

Flashes bright like shooting stars,
Illuminate our hidden scars.
Every echo, every gleam,
Guides us to our waking dream.

In the depths, we seek our peace,
Where the luminous never cease.
Life and love in rhythm, sweep,
Luminous echoes of the deep.

Secrets of the Starlit Chasm

Twinkling lights in velvet skies,
Whisper tales of long-lost ties.
Secrets swirl in cosmic dance,
Fateful dreams of love's expanse.

Beneath the stars, the shadows play,
Hiding truths that fade away.
Crimson skies and midnight's call,
Enigmas lurk and spirits fall.

Through the chasm, hope's light beams,
Illuminating silent dreams.
Every star a wish, a fate,
Secrets woven, hearts await.

Orbs of silver, depths unknown,
Guiding lost souls, all alone.
In this vast, enchanted dark,
Every whisper leaves a mark.

Secrets sealed in timeless space,
Chasing echoes, we embrace.
In the starlit chasm's hold,
Stories written, yet untold.

Glimmers in the Bottomless Dark

In the void where fears unite,
Glimmers spark in endless night.
Faintly shining, shadows weave,
Truth and hope we dare believe.

Endless depths, a quiet song,
Voices rise where dreams belong.
Every glimmer, soft and shy,
A beacon beckons from the sky.

Through the dark, we search for light,
Navigating endless night.
Every moment, a heartbeat's dance,
In this chasm, fate's romance.

Whispers linger, secrets swirl,
Glimmers twist in fate's grand whirl.
Holding on to fragile dreams,
In the dark, our spirit gleams.

In the bottomless dark we find,
Glimmers of a heart entwined.
Every spark a gentle guide,
Through the night, we shall abide.

Reflections in the Void

In shadows deep, where silence sways,
The echoes dance in faded rays.
A canvas blank, a mind untamed,
In whispered thoughts, we're all unnamed.

Fragments lost in timeless night,
Each moment fades, yet feels so bright.
We seek a truth in empty space,
But find our fears in their embrace.

The stars above, they seem so near,
Yet in the dark, we drown in fear.
Reflections clash, then softly blend,
In infinite realms where shadows bend.

A mirror breaks, the shards unite,
Each piece a tale of silent plight.
We search for sense amidst the chaos,
In voids of thought, we sometimes stray us.

Yet in this dance of light and shade,
A fragile thread, our hopes conveyed.
Through all the silence, hear the call,
In echoes deep, we rise and fall.

Depths of Infinite Echoes

In caverns dark, where whispers dwell,
The echoes rise, a haunting spell.
Each sound a tale, a life once known,
Resounding deep, in hearts they've sown.

The currents pull, we drift and dive,
In depths unknown, we feel alive.
Each echo lingers, soft and clear,
A melody of love and fear.

Through endless waves, our voices blend,
In harmony, we start to mend.
Beyond the void, where dreams reside,
In infinite echoes, we confide.

Yet still we yearn, for brighter skies,
To break the chains and realize.
In echoes vast, our spirits soar,
To depths unknown, forevermore.

With every sound, a chance to grow,
In whispered waves, our truths bestow.
In depths of echoes, we shall find,
Reflections of the heart and mind.

Shattered Glass of Forever

In realms where light and shadow meet,
Fractured dreams lie at our feet.
Each shard reflects a distant past,
A moment held, yet fading fast.

Crimson hues in broken lines,
Whispers dwell in dark designs.
The world is cracked, yet still it glows,
In shattered glass, our spirit flows.

We trace the edges, sharp and true,
Through cuts and pain, we find our view.
In scattered pieces, hope ignites,
As beauty blooms in darkest nights.

Forever echoes in our hearts,
In cracks we mend, the light imparts.
Though shattered glass may wound and scar,
It holds the light of who we are.

Each broken dream, a path revealed,
In chaos, strength is often sealed.
Like jewels that shine through tears we shed,
In shattered glass, our stories spread.

Whispers from the Abyssal Depths

From shadows deep, a voice ascends,
In whispered tones, the darkness blends.
An ancient song, a lullaby,
In depths unknown, where secrets lie.

The ocean breathes a timeless hymn,
In swirling currents, dark and grim.
Yet in the depths, a spark persists,
With every wave, a chance to exist.

Beneath the surface, dreams collide,
In tides of grief, we learn to ride.
In whispers soft, the heart takes flight,
Emerging from the dark of night.

Through murky waters, we may drown,
Yet hope will guide us, pull us 'round.
In abyssal depths, we'll seek the light,
Through whispered fears, we rise in might.

The echoes fade, but still we hear,
In quietude, we face our fear.
From depths unseen, we choose to rise,
In whispers soft, we touch the skies.

On the Edge of the Abyss

I stand where the light fades away,
A whisper of hope in the fray.
The chasm beneath calls my name,
Daring me to play its dark game.

The winds tell tales of lost souls,
Chasing dreams that darkness controls.
With every step, the void draws near,
Where echoes of silence stoke fear.

Yet courage flickers like a light,
Against the cold grip of the night.
I breathe in deep, my heart a drum,
For in this abyss, I shall not succumb.

What lies below, I cannot know,
But a part of me longs to go.
To uncover secrets of the deep,
In the depths where shadows creep.

So here I stand on the brink of fate,
With each heartbeat, I hesitate.
But something stirs within my soul,
To leap into the infinite whole.

Fragments of a Forsaken Reflection

Mirrors shatter, dreams collide,
Whispers lost in time abide.
Each shard a piece of what was whole,
A haunting testament to the soul.

In darkened corners, memories shine,
Fleeting visions, lost in time.
Promises broken, echoes fade,
In quiet chambers, shadows invade.

Faces flicker, stories untold,
Grief envelopes, a grip so cold.
Sifting through the dust of despair,
Finding pieces that once were there.

Fragments glimmer like stars in night,
A map to navigate the fight.
I gather the remnants, one by one,
Rebuilding a past that's come undone.

Yet in this search, a truth appears,
Through the sorrow, through the fears.
A reflection forged in pain's embrace,
Shows beauty resides in each frayed space.

Shadows That Speak

In corners dark, the silence breathes,
Shadows gather, weaving leaves.
Voices echo in subtle tones,
Stories whispered from ancient bones.

They beckon forth, these shades of yore,
With secrets held behind closed doors.
They dance in rhythms, soft and low,
Crafting tales of ebb and flow.

Each silhouette a life once lived,
Echoing the love they give.
Lost in twilight's gentle embrace,
I seek the warmth within their space.

As darkness weaves its veiled intent,
These murmurs carry a sacred scent.
They guide my heart, the path to take,
In shadows deep, new truths awake.

So listen close, to what they say,
In the quiet of the fading day.
For in their form, the past doth stay,
Shadows that speak, in night's ballet.

Into the Abyssal Unknown

I stand at doors of dreams and dread,
Where light meets dark, and angels tread.
The abyss calls with haunting grace,
Inviting me to find my place.

What lies beyond this fragile veil?
A journey forged of hope and frail.
I sense the pull of the unfathomed deep,
Where secrets lie and lost souls weep.

A shiver dances on my skin,
As I ponder what waits within.
Will I emerge, or be forever lost,
In echoes of fate, counting the cost?

Every heartbeat weighs like stone,
While shadows flicker, chill and moan.
Yet still I feel the call anew,
To plunge where few have dared to view.

The unknown beckons with strength untold,
A story waiting to unfold.
With every breath, I step outside,
Into the abyss, where dreams abide.

Phantoms in the Infinite Pool

In the water's glassy gaze,
Whispers echo, soft and low.
Figures dance in fleeting haze,
Dreams and shadows come and go.

Ripples part the silent night,
Stars are captured, twinkling bright.
Fingers trace the surface light,
Lost in visions, taking flight.

Beneath the moon's pale embrace,
Lies a world, a hidden space.
Phantoms swim with ghostly grace,
Waves of time, a slow, soft chase.

Ebb and flow the memories,
Caught in tides of destiny.
Voices call from in the breeze,
Calling forth their melody.

In this realm where waters speak,
Secrets shared, the bold and weak.
Nature's mirror, fate's mystique,
In the pool, the lost all seek.

Through the Looking Abyss

Gaze into the darkening glass,
Reflections twist and warp the view.
Shapes emerge, then fade like grass,
In shadows deep, the thoughts ensue.

What lies beyond this shrouded line?
Starlit whispers loom and sway.
Time stands still, a hidden sign,
Launches forth where echoes play.

Eyes of night, they pierce the veil,
What secrets lurk beneath the calm?
Haunting tunes weave serpents' trail,
In silence there, we seek the balm.

Through the void, a chilling sound,
Guides the way for souls forlorn.
In the depths, where lost are found,
Veils of truth and dreams are worn.

Listen close; the abyss calls,
To brave the dark with hearts aglow.
In its depths, where silence falls,
Shadows dance, and whispers flow.

The Depths Unveiled

Underneath the shadowed tide,
Lies a realm beyond the known.
Secrets where the wonders hide,
In the deep where time has flown.

Coral halls and realms of blue,
Speak of journeys long and vast.
Every turn reveals the new,
Whispers of the ancient past.

Echoes drift like drifting sand,
In this world where dreams collide.
Fingers touch the ocean's hand,
Lost in currents, we abide.

Crimson rays of sunlight beam,
Through the waves, a tender flash.
Painting visions, bold as dreams,
In the depths where colors clash.

Unveiled now, this watery space,
Calls the hearts of bold and meek.
Treasures dwell in every trace,
In the depths, our souls may seek.

Ciphers of the Bottomless Silence

In the stillness, secrets bloom,
Whispers form in quiet shade.
Ciphers trace the edge of gloom,
Simple notes that never fade.

Listen close to silence deep,
Here, the shadows softly speak.
In their arms, the lost will weep,
Reading words that fate might seek.

Tides of stillness, wrapped in dark,
Hold the echoes of the past.
Each soft breath ignites a spark,
In the void, our shadows cast.

Dreams entwine in mystic prose,
Crafting tales of endless night.
Through the stillness, wisdom flows,
Glimmers shine with hidden light.

Ciphers dance within the silence,
Voices rise, then drift away.
In this hush, we find compliance,
Lessons learned in quiet play.

Chasms of the Unseen

In shadows deep, where echoes play,
Whispers linger, lost in gray.
Fathoms call of silent fears,
Boundless depths drown unseen tears.

Unraveled threads weave tales untold,
In the dark, the heart grows bold.
Yearning souls reach through the night,
Grasping dreams, they chase the light.

Haunting whispers stir the air,
In the void, a hidden glare.
A delicate dance of hope and dread,
Chasms breathe where angels tread.

Silent moons watch over all,
Marking time, both rise and fall.
From the shadows, spark a gleam,
Through the chasms, find the dream.

With every breath that dares to sing,
From the depths, a new voice springs.
In the unseen, futures weave,
And in the dark, we dare to believe.

The Illusion of the Infinite

Stars may shine with endless grace,
Yet in truth, they're not a trace.
Waves of light in fleeting span,
Crafting worlds with a flick of hand.

Infinity echoes in the vast,
Moments linger, yet slip past.
Fleeting shadows blend and twine,
A dance of time that feels divine.

Hopes ascend like whispers high,
Drifting softly through the sky.
Yet horizons fade beyond the sight,
Lost in depths of endless night.

Through the veil of dreams we roam,
Chasing feelings that feel like home.
Elusive paths, we try to find,
Through the illusion, all entwined.

In every heart, a flicker stays,
Of boundless love in countless ways.
Yet in shadows, truths reside,
Beneath the moon's celestial tide.

Secrets in the Shattered Glass

Fragments glimmer, lost in sights,
Holding whispers of past nights.
Through the cracks, reflections fall,
Echoes tell the stories small.

Each shard a tale, a moment missed,
A touch of joy, a fleeting kiss.
Glimmers of laughter, shadows cast,
In broken dreams, the die is cast.

What remains in the scattered light?
Shadows dance, igniting night.
From the shards, we seek the whole,
Through the pain, we grasp the soul.

In silence stirs the heart's embrace,
Searching deep for a safe place.
Within the pieces lies the truth,
In shattered whispers, we find youth.

Through the chaos, beauty grows,
In every cut, the spirit flows.
Secrets dwell in angles so vast,
In shattered dreams, we hold the past.

Reflections of the Nameless

In mirrored depths, we lose our form,
Echoes whisper, dreams are born.
Faces fade like morning mist,
In the night, they weave and twist.

Silent stories gently creep,
Through fading light, the shadows seep.
A canvas bare, yet colors dance,
In the stillness, we take a chance.

Time reveals the hidden face,
Behind the masks, a sacred space.
With every glance, we glimpse the whole,
Reflections stir the searching soul.

Nameless wonders, lost in time,
Finding rhythm, losing rhyme.
In the silence, truths collide,
With each heartbeat, worlds inside.

Yet in this dance of fading light,
We seek the names that feel so right.
In the reflections, we find grace,
In the nameless, we embrace.

Phantoms of the Endless Gaze

Whispers float on midnight's breath,
Shadows dance beneath the stars,
Eyes that watch yet cannot see,
Lost within their silent scars.

Figures glide through foggy dreams,
Veils of gray obscure their forms,
Each a tale of yesteryears,
Painted in the tried and worn.

Moonlight glimmers on their paths,
Casting doubts upon the night,
Phantoms murmur secrets deep,
Fleeting flickers, out of sight.

In the stillness, echoes stir,
Every breath a lingering call,
Memories wrapped in shadows tight,
Where the ancient whispers fall.

Lost in echoes, time stands still,
Carried through the endless maze,
In the silence, we await,
Phantoms of the endless gaze.

In the Wake of the Abyss

Waves crash down in moonlit rage,
The ocean swallows the faint cries,
Whirlpools pull the lost below,
In darkness where the mystery lies.

Voices rise like sirens' songs,
Echoing through tempest's roar,
Haunting whispers of the deep,
Enticing souls from distant shore.

Clutching shadows, time is lost,
In the depths where dreams collide,
In the wake of the abyss,
Life's fleeting warmth is cast aside.

Ghostly figures dance in foam,
As waters claim those who stray,
In the struggle, hope is dimmed,
In the night where visions fray.

Yet beneath the swirling dark,
A glimmer seeks the morning light,
In the wake of the abyss,
We chase the dawn, prepared to fight.

Echoes of the Unfathomable

In the cavern of the mind,
Thoughts cascade like distant stars,
Silent screams in endless night,
Carried forth on drifting cars.

Layers deep of hidden tales,
Unraveled threads pull at the core,
Each faint echo, memory's mark,
Of adventures nevermore.

Void of certainty, hope and dread,
Dance together in whispered hymns,
Ethereal strings of sound and sight,
Intertwined like faded dreams.

Through the dark, the pulse does beat,
As shadows flicker and entwine,
Echoes call from depths unknown,
Where the boundaries blur and shine.

In the silence, storms may rise,
Bringing clarity to the fight,
In the echoes of the unfathomable,
We awaken, reaching for the light.

Reflections of the Darkened Heart

Mirrors cracked beneath the weight,
Of secrets never meant to stay,
Shards of life, they weave the tale,
Of love and loss in disarray.

Each reflection tells a story,
Faded hopes and dreams once bright,
Darkened hues of echoing pain,
Glimmer softly in the night.

Comfort lingers in the gloom,
Where shadows cast their fleeting dreams,
Yearning hearts read in the dark,
What was lost, or so it seems.

Through the windows of the soul,
Light peeks in to heal the scars,
Reflections linger, dance and sway,
Beneath the backdrop of the stars.

Embrace the pain, let it be known,
As whispers fade, new paths may start,
In the shadows of the past,
We find ourselves, and heal the heart.

Visions from the Depths Beyond

In swirling mists where secrets blend,
A whisper calls, the shadows bend.
Colors swirl, a dance of light,
Dreams awaken, through the night.

Beneath the waves, a story sleeps,
Ancient echoes, silence keeps.
Visions flicker, soft and clear,
Mysterious figures drawing near.

From the depths, a voice does rise,
Questions woven in the skies.
Revealing paths that few have known,
Footprints marked, yet all alone.

Glimmers flick through tangled dreams,
Beneath the surface, not as it seems.
Memories dance, fade and glow,
As tides of time begin to flow.

Open your heart, let visions guide,
Through depths where shadows reside.
In the darkness, truth will blend,
In dreams, beginnings find their end.

Veils of Time in the Night's Embrace

Under stars, the night unfolds,
Whispers soft of tales told.
The moonlight weaves through trees so tight,
Veils of time in silver light.

Moments linger, sweet and slow,
Secrets in the breezes blow.
Footsteps soft on paths of dreams,
In silent echoes, starlight gleams.

A cradle held in twilight's grip,
Time and space begin to slip.
Laughter fades, yet shadows dance,
In this realm of fleeting chance.

Fleeting visions drift and sway,
In the embrace of night, they play.
Histories wrapped in twilight's lace,
In endless wonders, find our place.

From depths of time, we seek to learn,
In every heartbeat, passions burn.
So let the night, in whispers, speak,
Through veils of time, it's truth we seek.

Lost in the Labyrinth of Shadows

In the maze where darkness dwells,
Echoes of forgotten bells.
Whispers call, with voices low,
Guiding steps where few dare go.

Twisting paths, a mirror's gaze,
Reflections lost in foggy haze.
Each turn brings a brand-new face,
Shadows shift, then fade in grace.

In the depths, secrets intertwine,
A dance of fate, a quest for time.
Every breath a path unknown,
Together lost, yet still alone.

Light flickers, a challenge bold,
Through the chill, the heart feels cold.
In this labyrinth, dreams collide,
Finding hope where shadows bide.

Yet through the dark, a spark ignites,
Guiding lost souls through the nights.
In every corner, chance awaits,
For those who seek to change their fates.

The Abyss Gazes Back

Into the void where silence reigns,
Questions swirl like hidden chains.
Glimpses of fate in shadows deep,
Awakening secrets we must keep.

Stare not too long, the abyss breathes,
Inviting those who dare to seize.
An echo forms in depths of black,
For every soul that turns its back.

Through swirling night, we seek the truth,
The remnants lost of fearless youth.
In haunting whispers, wisdom speaks,
Revealing strength when courage peaks.

Yet know this well, the darkness knows,
The deepest fears, where madness grows.
A dance of thoughts within the mind,
For those who gaze, the past is blind.

Embrace the dark and all it brings,
For in the void, the heart takes wings.
Explore the depths where shadows play,
In silence found, we find our way.

Reflections in the Infinite Void

In the stillness of the night,
Stars whisper their ancient tales,
Mirrored in the vast expanse,
A dance where silence prevails.

Thoughts drift like drifting clouds,
Lost in a sea of endless dreams,
Each one a fragment of me,
Flowing through cosmic streams.

In shadows deep and secrets old,
The universe wraps me tight,
Every pulse a tale retold,
In the cradle of starlight.

Thoughts collide, yet softly fade,
Echoes in the void align,
Time slips through a gentle shade,
Infinite, yet so divine.

Here I stand, a fleeting spark,
In the canvas of the night,
Reflections of a cosmic arc,
A whisper lost in flight.

Echoes of the Endless Depths

Deep beneath the ocean's sway,
Voices murmur, faint and far,
Ripples cradle night and day,
Guided by the distant stars.

Waves caress the sunken dreams,
Lost in tides that never sleep,
Carrying their haunting beams,
Secrets that the waters keep.

In the realm of shadows cast,
Echoes dance through liquid glass,
Memories of moments past,
Whispers of a time that has.

Submerged in hues of gentle blue,
All the world feels soft and light,
Every surge brings visions new,
In the depths of endless night.

Here I wander, lost yet free,
Among the echoes of the deep,
In the depths, a mystery,
Awake while others sleep.

Shadows in the Abyssal Glass

In the mirror of the night,
Shadows shift and softly blend,
Each reflection holds a light,
In the depths where visions mend.

Among the whispers, secrets lie,
Formless shapes that swirl and glide,
Dancing to a silent sigh,
Where all lost hopes abide.

Buried deep, memories pulse,
Fragile as the air we breathe,
Every heartbeat, every impulse,
Awakens dreams we dare believe.

In this glass of dreams and fears,
Timeless shadows oft will roam,
Carved from laughter, woven tears,
Finding solace in their home.

As the abyss unveils its face,
I reflect upon each thread,
In the silence, find my place,
In shadows where I have tread.

Whispers of the Boundless Night

Underneath a blanket dark,
Stars emerge like distant sighs,
Each one bears a spark,
Of dreams whispered from the skies.

In the stillness, silence hums,
Crickets play their timeless tune,
Every heartache slowly succumbs,
To the magic of the moon.

Softly glide across the night,
The breeze carries tales untold,
Each whisper cloaked in pure delight,
Traces of the brave and bold.

Moments weave into the dark,
Echoes of laughter, sighs, and tears,
In this space, we leave our mark,
While facing all our hidden fears.

Beneath the vast, eternal dome,
Every star becomes a guide,
In the darkness, we find home,
In the night, we learn to bide.

Beneath the Veil of Shadows

In twilight's grip, the silence breathes,
A world concealed in whispered leaves.
Secrets dance in the waning light,
Beneath the veil, where shadows ignite.

The moon unfolds her silver lace,
In hidden paths, we find our space.
Echoes of dreams begin to call,
In this dark realm, we rise and fall.

The night holds stories yet untold,
Of hearts entwined and spirits bold.
Beneath the whispers of ancient trees,
We find our truth, our gentle peace.

With every breath, the darkness sighs,
A symphony beneath the skies.
Together we tread this mystic ground,
Where courage blooms and fears unbound.

So linger here, where shadows play,
In the space where night meets day.
For in the dark, we may discover,
The light within, like no other.

The Infinite Inward Journey

Through the chamber of the soul we glide,
Adrift on currents, where dreams reside.
Each thought a lantern, shining bright,
Guiding us through the endless night.

In valleys low and mountains high,
We seek the stars within the sky.
With every step, we lose and find,
The depths of heart, the shape of mind.

Reflections dance in a crystal sphere,
Whispers carry what we hold dear.
The journey inward, vast and wide,
Unveils the truth we cannot hide.

Time bends here, a gentle stream,
Flowing softly, like a dream.
Each layer peeled, a new surprise,
Unlocks the door to the skies.

In this vast ocean of the self,
We gather wisdom, like timeless wealth.
A tapestry of light appears,
Woven threads of hopes and fears.

Whispers of the Cosmic Chasm

In the void where silence reigns,
Echoes of existence flow through veins.
Stars collide in celestial dance,
In the chasm deep, we take our chance.

Beneath the vast and endless sea,
A chorus sings of what could be.
Galaxies twirl, a cosmic play,
Whispers of night that guide our way.

With every heartbeat, worlds collide,
In the chasm, we choose to hide.
Yet courage stirs in darkest places,
Summoning light through all the faces.

The universe breathes a soothing tune,
A reminder of life beneath the moon.
We venture forth, into the unknown,
With the stars as our guides, never alone.

From the depths, we rise anew,
Carried forth on the cosmic blue.
In the whispers of the void's embrace,
We discover a sacred space.

The Night's Deep Embrace

In the twilight's soft and tender fold,
The night unveils her secrets bold.
Wrapped in shadows, we lose our name,
In the silence, we fan the flame.

Stars ignite in a velvet sky,
While dreams take flight and softly sigh.
The moon watches with a knowing grace,
As we dance in the night's warm embrace.

With every shadow, a story unfolds,
Whispers of love in the night retold.
Through the darkness, we find our way,
Guided by the night, come what may.

Waves of peace on the winds do swell,
Cradling hearts in the night's gentle spell.
Together we wander, hand in hand,
In the deep embrace, we understand.

Each moment glows, a treasure to hold,
As the night wraps us in dreams untold.
In the sanctuary of starlit grace,
We find our home in the night's embrace.

Abyssal Symphonies

In shadows deep, the whispers play,
A haunting tune, night turns to day.
Echoes of dreams, lost in the sea,
Drifting softly, they call to me.

Beneath the waves, where silence dwells,
The heartbeats sound like distant bells.
Melodies weave through the darkened blue,
Crafting stories, old yet new.

Fathoms swirl with secrets untold,
Notes of the past, vibrant and bold.
As currents shift and shadows shift,
In depths unknown, the spirits lift.

A symphony born of the night,
Guides lost souls toward the light.
Together we dance, in mystic embrace,
Eternal echoes, our sacred space.

Through the abyss, we find our grace,
In every note, a warm embrace.
A melody deep, where we belong,
In abyssal symphonies, we are strong.

Eclipsed Realities

Under the veil of a cosmic sigh,
Lies a world where shadows lie.
Dreamers wander through fractured light,
Chasing whispers, lost in night.

Aligned with stars, fate's gentle hand,
Eclipses draw lines through distant land.
Veils of truth, woven in lore,
Guard the secrets of evermore.

Fields of doubt stretch far and wide,
Yet beneath the surface, we confide.
Eyes closed tight, we seek to find,
The echoes of a dreaming mind.

Here in the hush, where silence reigns,
Eclipsed realities break the chains.
Great mysteries call in a single breath,
Awakening life amidst the death.

A paradox spun in twilight's kiss,
Reveals the heart's forgotten bliss.
In shadows cast, our truths ignite,
Into the dark, we step, take flight.

Spirals into the Depths

Spirals weave into the night,
Drawing me close, beyond the light.
In gentle turns, I lose my way,
Into the dark, I long to stay.

Beneath the surface, feelings grow,
Emotions swell like tides that flow.
Whirlpools spin, a dance so bold,
In the embrace of hidden gold.

Each twist reveals a tale untold,
Life's mysteries in darkness unfold.
A journey deep, where secrets breathe,
Leads minds to wonder, hearts to seethe.

Tethered tightly, yet wanting more,
Curious souls dive to explore.
In swirling depths, we find our peace,
In spirals, our burdens cease.

From abyssal truths, we rise anew,
Discovering paths, hearts breaking through.
Together, we spiral, hand in hand,
Exploring the depths of this uncharted land.

Reflected Longing in the Dark

In quiet rooms where echoes fade,
Reflected dreams begin to wade.
Longing glimmers in every sigh,
Like distant stars that fill the sky.

Mirrors show what hearts conceal,
Desires dance and softly heel.
Loneliness hums a tender tune,
Beneath the watchful, watching moon.

Every shadow holds its place,
Hiding love with a stoic face.
Yet yearning spills, a flood of grace,
In the dark, we find our space.

Soft whispers brush against my soul,
Carving paths, making me whole.
Through longing eyes, we dare to dream,
Finding solace in the gleam.

In twilight's breath, the truth ignites,
Reflected glances spark the nights.
In the dark, what once was lost,
Finds rebirth, despite the cost.

Dancers Beneath the Celestial Veil

Beneath the stars they twirl and glide,
Whispers of night their only guide.
In silent shadows, dreams take flight,
Dancers weave magic in the moonlight.

With every turn, the cosmos sways,
Embracing the music of their plays.
Galaxies shimmer in eyes so bright,
Uniting in harmony, pure delight.

Their laughter echoes through the night,
A symphony formed by soft starlight.
Together they paint the sky anew,
With hues of love in every view.

Beneath the veil of celestial glow,
The mysteries of dance begin to flow.
Each step, a story, each leap, a tale,
In this eternal, enchanted trail.

So let the heavens witness this art,
As stars bear witness to every heart.
Dancers beneath the celestial dome,
Finding in the universe, their home.

The Infinite's Reckoning

In the depths of time, shadows collide,
As the universe breathes, far and wide.
Echoes of moments stretch and bend,
Marking the path where cycles end.

Stars forget their origin's grace,
Counting the beats of the time and space.
Infinite whispers in voids confide,
Reckoning lives destined to hide.

Each heartbeat a chapter, lost then found,
In galaxies where the silence resounds.
Time's relentless march knows no cease,
Yet cradles existence in gentle peace.

The cosmos sprawls with stories untold,
In silence, the infinite slowly unfolds.
A tapestry woven with threads of fate,
Binding the universe, never too late.

As stardust emerges from ages past,
The reckoning waits, silent and vast.
In the vastness, we learn to embrace,
The infinite truth of our sacred space.

Reflections of Forgotten Souls

In the quiet hollow of the night,
Whispers linger, fading from sight.
Reflections dance in silver pools,
Memories bound by destiny's rules.

Forgotten souls in echoing haze,
Lost in the labyrinth of time's maze.
They seek the warmth of a distant dawn,
Finding solace when shadows have drawn.

Each glance a story, laden with pain,
Echoes of laughter, remnants of gain.
Through the mist of silence they roam,
Seeking the fragments of a lost home.

Still they remember, though lost, alone,
Flickers of joy in the heart like stone.
In the twilight where old dreams dwell,
The reflections whisper their silent spell.

For every spirit that drifts away,
There blooms a universe, tender as clay.
In reflections, we gather, we bind,
The forgotten souls, eternally intertwined.

Portals to the Unseen Realms

Beneath the veil of what we know,
Portals shimmer, inviting us to go.
Through the secret paths of light and shade,
Unseen realms beckon, unafraid.

With eyes closed tight, we drift away,
Dancing through dimensions where shadows play.
Whispers of worlds we yearn to see,
In the depths of cosmic mystery.

Every step taken, a passage defined,
In the echoes of time, our hearts aligned.
Cascades of magic, soft as a dream,
Awaken the wonders that silently gleam.

In these realms we find timeless flight,
Exploring the canvas of endless night.
Crafting connections with threads unseen,
In the embrace of what might have been.

So journey forth into the unknown,
For every portal leads to a throne.
In the unseen, our spirits can soar,
Discovering treasures forevermore.

www.ingramcontent.com/pod-product-compliance
Ingram Content Group UK Ltd.
Pitfield, Milton Keynes, MK11 3LW, UK
UKHW021420230125
4262UKWH00028B/376